Jean,

May you live
your word!

Laura Gunion

living word

What one word defines you?

by Laura E. Gentry
photographs by William F. Gentry II

acknowledgments

We extend our heartfelt thanks to all of the *Living Word* participants. Your creativity, thoughtfulness, and enthusiasm are what make these portraits so compelling. We acknowledge Luther College, Decorah, Iowa, for providing so many participants and allowing us to shoot photographs in their Center for the Arts, and Professor Carol Gilbertson for featuring *Living Word* at a Poetry Project event on campus. We would also like to thank our parents, Burnell and Sharon Smith, and Verona and the late William Gentry, for their enduring love and support.

Editors: Dwayne M. and Joan Liffring-Zug Bourret, Maureen Patterson, Dorothy Crum, Melinda Bradnan, and Julie Eisele
Graphic Designer: Molly Cook, M.A. Cook Design

Exhibitions and prints of *Living Word* photographs are available.
To host a *Living Word* event, contact the Gentrys
at lauragentry@lycos.com

Books By Mail (2005 prices subject to change)
Living Word, this book, $14.95
Custom-printed T-shirt with your word $14.95
    (please specify size: YL, S, M, L, XL, 2X, 3X)
Shipping and handling to one address $5.95
Iowans add 5% state sales tax
Send postpaid orders to:
Living Word
P.O. Box 11
Marquette, Iowa 52158
On-line ordering available at www.thegentryjoint.com
or call Penfield Books 1-800-728-9998 for books only

© 2005 William and Laura Gentry
Library of Congress 2005902902
ISBN 1-932043-32-2

The passion flower graces the *Living Word* logo. This flowering Latin American vine was named for the Passion—the suffering and death of Jesus Christ. Many features of this plant suggest aspects of the crucifixion, such as the circle of hair-like rays emanating from the center that resemble Christ's crown of thorns and the three stigmata, which look like the nails used to crucify Him. The Gentrys chose this flower to be the icon of these portraits because Jesus Christ is the very Living Word of God, who has shown us how to live fully, passionately.

about the gentrys

Shown on the front cover, William and Laura Gentry are artists and pastors living and working in Northeast Iowa. Both attended seminary in Berkeley, California, where they were married in 1996. They are passionate about using their gifts in the arts to bring about spiritual growth and awareness.

Born and raised in Alaska, William is minister of the First Congregational Churches of McGregor and Elkader, Iowa. He holds a bachelor of arts degree in philosophy from Regis University in Denver, Colorado. He studied at Harvard Divinity School and Pacific School of Religion in Berkeley, where he earned a master of divinity degree.

A native to Iowa, Laura is minister of Waterville Lutheran Church in Waterville and Our Savior's Lutheran Church in Lansing. She holds a bachelor of arts degree in art, theater, and dance from Luther College in Decorah, Iowa. From Pacific School of Religion, she holds a master of divinity and a master of arts in the area of "worship and the arts."

The Gentrys draw inspiration from their ministries and from the natural beauty of the Mississippi River valley in which they live. To learn more and view their latest works, visit their website at www.thegentryjoint.com.

contents

introduction..2
foreword..5

parts of speech

adjectives..6
adverbs..68
conjunctions...71
nouns..74
preposition...106
verbs...108

epilogue

one-on-one conversations..120
group conversations..120
party games...121

introduction

By Laura E. Gentry

"What one word defines you?" If you had to express the complex essence of your identity in just one word, what would it be? In order to create the artwork in this collection, we asked this question to more than one hundred people.

For years as a couple, we have both said that we suffer from *and* trouble: we are constantly adding new things to our lives. One day, when we were pondering what kind of photographic series William might try next, I suggested that he do some unusual self-portraits. He joked, "What do you want me to do? Take a picture of myself in a T-shirt that says 'and?'" We threw our heads back in laughter that soon gave way to serious conversation about the creative possibilities of this innovative idea.

Portraits are compelling because faces are storytellers. Researchers have discovered that a whole section of the human brain is dedicated to recognizing facial gestures—giving us the remarkable ability to discern at least seven thousand different expressions. For this reason, we intuitively seek human connection in others' faces, even if that face is but a photograph or painting. A portrait can allow viewers to feel that they know the subject, that they intimately understand the stranger in the picture.

These portraits, we decided, would include none of the accouterments that people ordinarily use to declare their status or uniqueness. These photographic portraits would be stripped down to the essential face and upper body in a white T-shirt against a black background, thus democratizing the exhibit. Then we would introduce a unique element: each subject would wear one word, inviting the audience to better understand his or her character. Our reasons for limiting the selection to one word were to emphasize the elegance of brevity and to aid in the overall visual simplicity of the portraits. Viewers' aesthetic experience would subtly guide their sense of the word's meaning—and this meaning would, in turn, affect their impressions of the person portrayed: each would make the other come alive.

Living Word is the title we gave to this exhibit. On a literal level, it suggests how much vitality words give to our lives. Each person, by wearing his or her word, brings it to life. As theologians, we also wanted the title to imply a relationship to the Word of God. As broken people looking for answers, we seek direction from our Creator—we long for God to speak a word of hope to us. It is the Bible, most often, which is considered to be the Word of God because it contains the writings of inspired writers who have faithfully documented God's messages to us. Nevertheless, the primary Word of God—the most evident way that Christians believe God has spoken the Word of Love to humanity—is through Jesus Christ himself. God did not simply send the scriptures to us; the God of the universe "became flesh and dwelt among us," as John's gospel proclaims. Jesus is the very living, breathing embodiment of God's Word.

And yet, there is an even more expansive understanding of the Word of God and this comes from the first chapter of Genesis. Here, God's words "Let there be . . ." result in the phenomena of creation. From this we can conclude that creation itself is the Word of God. Each and every aspect of this marvelous earth and her creatures is the Word of God. Therefore, we can say that we are each a Living Word from God.

What we are at birth is the gift from which we begin and from there unfurl our various identities. We live and breathe a message to the world through our every action. In calling this project *Living Word*, we are nudging people to think carefully about their very purpose in the world. What word do you live? What do you embody? As a miraculous Living Word of God, how do you bless the world by your existence?

Our participants wrestled with choices as they selected their words. They picked various parts of speech—adjectives, nouns, adverbs, conjunctions, verbs, and even a preposition—which is how we chose to organize this book. Some knew instantly what their word would be. Others wrote to reserve their spot in the show but could not come up with a word for several weeks, or would declare their choice and then write back a few days later with a different word. Still others sent a list of possible words and asked us to choose. We resisted the temptation to do so, explaining, "That's the whole point: you get to pick your own word—you define yourself in this exercise. It is meant to empower you."

Once the words were chosen, I painted them on the T-shirts. William shot many of the portraits in the atrium of Luther College's Center for the Arts, where students could observe us at work. One of the most enjoyable aspects of this process was talking with each participant during their photo shoot. Rather than having people pose, we fired off questions: "How did you choose your word? Why do you embody this word? Would others define you this way?" Though many of our subjects were strangers, they opened up to share their deeper truths. As the conversation progressed, we could see their countenance change. Talking about their words caused people to embody them. In those flashes of honesty and vulnerability, William captured many striking images, which often made the final selection difficult.

We still marvel at how many participants selected positive words to define themselves. We wondered if we had coincidentally happened upon a whole group of exceptionally happy people. As we thought about it, however, we realized it made perfect sense. Offering people the license to define themselves, rather than allowing others to define them, spurred them to think of themselves in the best light and to dream. Some of their words spoke of lofty ideals such as love, hope, and truth. These people admitted they couldn't possibly embody these words to their fullest extent, but they strive to live by them. Allowing people to define themselves, we learned, lifts peoples' sights beyond what they are to what they hope to be.

Now we invite you, our viewers, to "read" these portraits—to come to know these people and their words. It is our hope that they will cause you to consider your own identity—inviting you into richer, more intentional self-expression, that you too, may celebrate yourself as a Living Word.

foreword

By Dr. Richard Simon Hanson

Laura Gentry, along with her husband, William, are both artists and pastors. In Laura's college career, which is when I first met her, she concentrated her studies in the arts, combining visual art with theatre and dance. Those of us who were privileged to be her teachers saw Laura as both talented and energetic. Theological training did not diminish the artistic urges of either William or Laura. They have continued to be artists and have integrated art into their ministries, even practicing their artistic skills as a kind of ministry that extends beyond the parishes they serve as pastors. In the process they are daring to let their theology expand as well, so as to embrace the whole of human experience. They are as seriously pastoral in this pursuit as they are seriously artistic.

Theology in its narrowest sense is an impossible task, for the word implies the study of God. Inasmuch as God is beyond our comprehension, it is presumptuous to even try to think and speak beyond babbling ignorance. Yet two matters are possible and can be considered as within the realm of theology. One is to embrace and contemplate the manifold works of the Creator, the "words" that are the speech of creation. The other is to study relationships: how can we relate to God, that is, to the very source of our existence, and to the others who share our position as God's creatures, God's children? In our relating, each of us are words—words of response to our Creator and words of various messages to each other.

adjectives

wide-eyed

A college philosophy and Spanish major, *wide-eyed* spent a lot of time choosing this word. "I think this word reflects my curiosity," she explains, "my wonder at the world around me, and my residence in the perpetual, wide-eyed state of wanting to know about it."

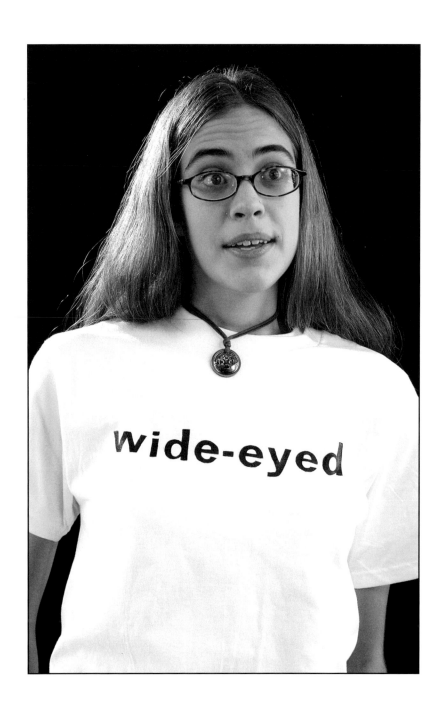

perky

Perky is an irresistibly upbeat and fun-loving farmer's wife who was hard-pressed to come up with a more accurate description of herself than "perky."

sassy

Like her twin sister *perky*, *sassy* is a happy-go-lucky person. "Sassy" means vigorous, lively, cheery, and saucy. This is definitely the word for a peppy secretary who keeps everyone on their toes.

possible

As a pastor and assistant to the bishop, *possible* helps congregations in need throughout the region. Her relentless optimism, know-how, and faith drive her belief that with God, all things are possible.

blessed

It is with grace and humility that *blessed* expresses her understanding of herself as imminently loved by God. All that she is and has is a blessing and she aims to bless others in return.

adjectives

spirited

Spirited is Wisconsin Public Radio's Distinguished Senior Broadcaster and host of the program *Here on Earth*. In 1990, her nationally syndicated series *Women of Spirit,* which consisted of five docudramas profiling the lives of extraordinary women in the history of the early church, won the National Association of Catholic Broadcasters' Gabriel Award and the Ohio State Award. Inspired by the women of faith whose lives she explored in these broadcasts, she, too, strives to live a spirited life.

disoriented

Disoriented is a busy artist, mother, and the wife of *addictive*. She chose "disoriented" (and wore her shirt backwards) as a humorous way to describe how dizzyingly disorienting her relentless schedule can be.

addictive

Prolific glass blowers, *addictive* and his wife have artwork in galleries across the country and in Europe. The reason for their success? "I have an addictive personality," he admits. What better to be addicted to than art?

feisty

Educator, community activist, and author, *feisty's* background includes a rich and varied career experience centered on education, nonprofit management, community development, and gender issues. "The word 'feisty' captures my spunk," she says. "But I'm neither quarrelsome nor touchy about the little things in life that don't always go my way. I'm no diva! But I am passionate about making the world a better place. As far as I'm concerned, living in peace requires people to insist on justice. So I am willing to stand up for what I believe in."

feisty

This *feisty* also fights for causes with intensity. She delights in provoking conversation with her "feisty" shirt. "Every time I wore it to my women's book club, they would all shriek with laughter and demand 'feisty' shirts of their own." So, we got them shirts and captured the feistiness of their group in the photo on the title page.

enthusiastic

"Recognized as the senior statesman of American college choral music," as *The Lutheran* declares, *enthusiastic's* 57-year legacy at Luther College is one of "humility, service, and unparalleled musicianship." The root of "enthusiastic" means filled with spirit—a fitting description of someone whose wisdom and faith have touched thousands of lives.

biodegradable

Biodegradable's environmental concerns club discussed the *Living Word* project and, together, they came up with this word. The woman who first came up with "biodegradable" and claimed it ended up being unavailable for the photo shoot. "So she told me that I could have the word. I was concerned that I was taking something that was hers, but she gave it to me." Our project, we realized, had made words a commodity—the intangible word became a tangible thing that you could give away like a cherished gift.

mortal

A poet and professor, *mortal* explains: "Because we are caught in time, we make art to fix impressions, seize moments, and to leave a trace. As the poet Wallace Stevens wrote, 'Death is the mother of beauty.'"

perishable

A guitarist, *perishable* says, "I don't feel morbid about it, but I do keep the awareness of mortality about me. The fact that this particular experiment in consciousness isn't going to last forever and isn't central to the scheme of things is actually more liberating and comforting to me than it is depressing. Right now, I just happen to be on vacation from being interstellar dust!"

hopeful

Photographer, publisher, and member of the Iowa Women's Hall of Fame, *hopeful* has been called the "premiere Iowa woman photographer of the twentieth century." Of her word choice, she says, "I was hopeful as a child in the depression, as a child of divorce, through World War II, one divorce, and subsequent struggles as a woman for equality, always hoping tomorrow is better."

helpful

Hopeful's husband chose the word "helpful," explaining, "Since I was 15, I've been in the service industry helping people and training other people to be helpful. I've done it so long, it's become a habit."

ebullient

The director of student services at the Diversity Center of her college, *ebullient* says this of her living word: "I think the fact that I laugh a lot and very heartily; that I refuse to see obstacles, I see opportunities; that the students I interact with think of me as part clown, part mom; that there is always laughter coming from my office when students visit are reasons why I describe myself as 'ebullient.'"

adjectives

ancient

Ever since *ancient* was a child, she has been entranced by tales of ancient civilizations. "I feel most alive when I am in contact with ancient artifacts," she says, "and often wonder what will be left behind when our culture is no longer here. I chose 'ancient' as my word not only because I feel ancient myself, but because I believe that in preserving artifacts for our human past, we are saving priceless pieces of our collective selves."

enchanting

Reared on fairy tales, *enchanting,* a young journalist, found this word irresistible and chose it to playfully hint at her romanticized view of life.

serious

Believe it or not, *serious* is a funeral director. Nevertheless, he also performs as a clown. People always tell him that he's too serious. We seriously doubt that's the case.

charismatic

Dramatic and full of life, *charismatic* has a charming warmth and an infectious laugh. As a foreign student, her charisma has helped her assimilate and thrive.

adjectives

awesome

Awesome loves to use this word to describe things, but she also seeks to be awesome herself. To evoke awe is an amazing thing.

radiant

"We are called to live passionately, without apology or restraint, creating light out of the darkness in this world," says *radiant*. A certain inner beauty radiates out of her as she lives her life. A dancer, actor, student, daughter, sister, friend, thinker, and writer, she touches everyone with the faith, love, and hope that makes her radiant.

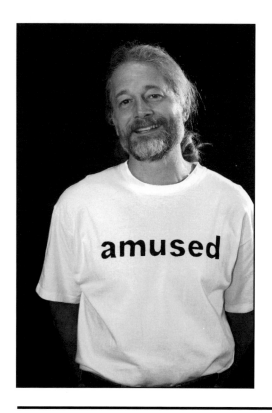

amused

A philosophy professor, *amused* says, "To be human is to get caught up in our own lives and to take ourselves and our projects very seriously. Yet at unexpected moments we may find ourselves stepping back from our busyness and looking upon our own scurrying about with a sense of detachment and amusement. As I have grown older, I've found myself overcome by this aura of amusement more often. In a way, we are absurd. For me, this absurdity has a lightness about it, unlike existential brooding. Aren't we humans silly, taking ourselves so seriously? Yet how could we be otherwise? It is amusing!"

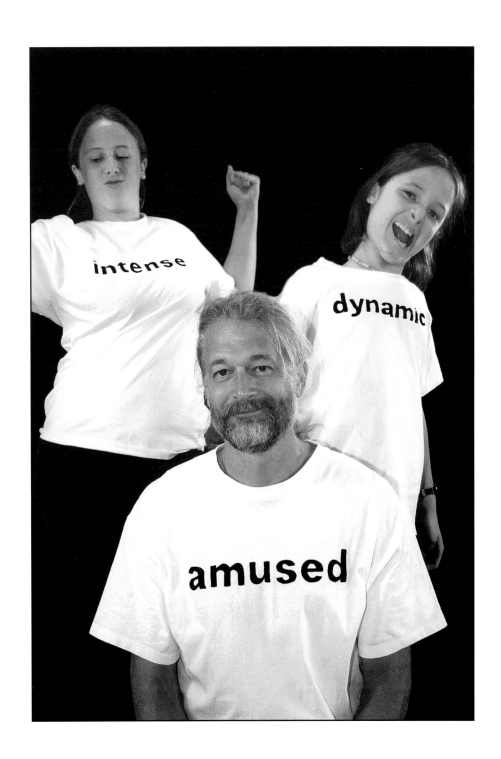

adjectives

intense

The older daughter of *amused*, *intense* has a passion for learning, acting, dancing, and for trying just about anything.

dynamic

Filled with drama and flare, *amused's* younger daughter, *dynamic,* is melodramatic, jubilant, and eager to express herself dynamically.

adjectives 37

one

At this point in her life, my niece knew how to answer the question "How old are you?" by emphatically holding up her finger and shouting, "One." Even the question, "Who are you?" she replied to by answering, "One." Therefore, we felt she was old enough to choose her own word for this project and this was, indeed, the one.

adjectives

hungry

"I am always hungry," says *hungry*. "Whether I am ordering a big steak or enjoying new experiences, some hungriness is being satiated. Life is an all-you-can-eat buffet, and I want to try a little bit of everything!"

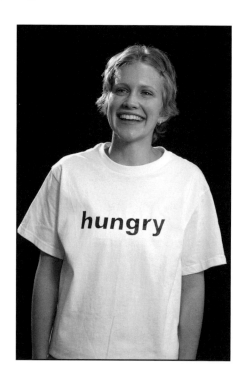

adventurous

Nothing stops *adventurous*. Even when her husband and daughter were stationed in Iraq at the same time, she did not lose heart, but kept up her adventurous spirit and took on the new challenge of being a nontraditional college student—making her a classmate of her son and daughter. Her favorite motto is "Behind the door marked 'fear' lies your greatest adventure."

vibrant

Youthful and energized, *vibrant's* dreams and goals are, indeed, bright. She says, "I like to believe that the glow I feel inside comes from the simple things in life, like the quietness of the first snowfall, or the joyous sounds of laughter. I can't help but share my bliss, and so my vibrant personality is fueled, in essence, by those around me."

vivacious

An artist, teacher, and youth volunteer, *vivacious* bounds around with creative energy and makes her art classes come alive. She says she chose this word because "I can't sit still, I sleep little, I think fast, talk fast, and I go with the moment."

curious

Inspired by the children's book character Curious George, with whom he shares a name, *curious* found this word most fitting. When he served as the Presiding Bishop of the Evangelical Lutheran Church in America, his curiosity was an invaluable asset—helping him to listen and learn tirelessly.

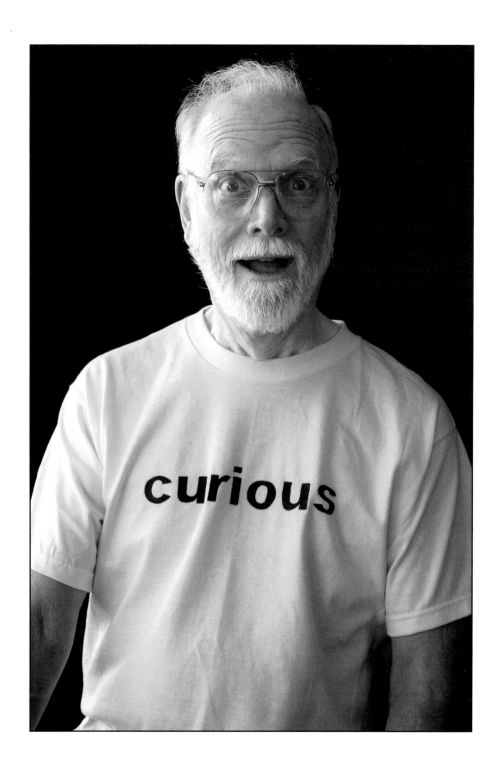

adjectives

liberated

Liberated writes this of herself in the third person: "Liberated from four walls without a door, at long last flying free. She's no longer gazing out that window. She's on her own, doing well, and finally living . . ."

strong

"In the three years since I left home," says *strong*, "I have had to deal with many difficult and painful situations. Each of these events deepened my strength and molded me into the person I am today: a woman with the entire world at her feet, who plans to explore every ounce of it."

brave

Creative and undaunted by most everything, *brave* is eager and willing to try just about anything.

adjectives

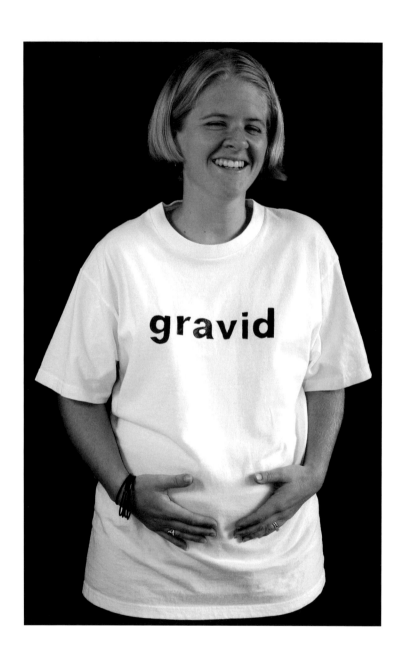

gravid

Gravid is a Norwegian word that means "with child, or heavy." During her pregnancy, *gravid,* a soccer coach, found that people didn't ask about her anymore—it was all about the baby. "There was no more 'me,' only 'us,'" she says. It is still that way, now that Larsson has been born, a beautiful baby boy who is the center of her world (instead of the center of her belly).

random

The word "random" refers to a haphazard course, without direction or rule. *Random* selected this adjective because of its freedom—how it is unbound by convention or logic. She strives to live in this fashion.

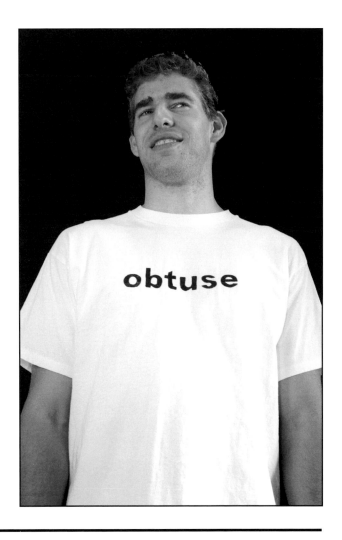

obtuse

"Clumsiness is a characteristic that plagues some of us our entire lives," says *obtuse* about his favorite word, "and the journey toward embracing that awkward part of us is endless."

bookish

Bookish, a professor and biblical scholar, is, indeed, a lover of books. She devours books of all genres and even admits to listening to novels on tape while reading another book or magazine at the same time. "I purposefully didn't wear my glasses today," she told us. "I don't think you have to look bookish to be bookish."

undecided

A college student without a declared major, *undecided* is the label her institution uses to describe her, and she thinks it is rather fitting. She is still undecided about a number of aspects of her life but finds great satisfaction in the journey toward self-discovery.

unique

Unique is also trying to figure out who she is. She feels she is "never an outcast but always different." *Unique* is truly one-of-a-kind.

free

A gifted musician and educator, *free* declares, "As a young adult maturing in the twenty-first century there are many paths my life could take. Which one I will take I have yet to decide, but I know the choice is mine, I'm free."

colorful

Colorful is an energetic student with a wide variety of interests and talents. She displays a most colorful personality.

tenacious

A bright young artist on her way to becoming a medical illustrator, *tenacious* holds firmly to her goals. She says that her tenacity is among her strongest assets, especially during her difficult studies.

jovial

When her friends hear hearty, robust laughter rolling down the hall, they know *jovial* is near. With relentless good humor and a positive attitude, *jovial* makes her way through life.

adjectives

kind

Conductor, composer, arranger, and music educator from the Dominican Republic, *kind* holds a PhD in music education, an associate degree in pedagogy of music theory, and a degree in electromechanical engineering. He has written and published many choral arrangements of Caribbean and Latin American music. During the past twenty-four years he has conducted choirs, bands, and orchestras in North America, Europe, and Central and South America. He served as a consultant for the design and implementation of the nation-wide music education curriculum in the Dominican Republic. Yet despite all these accomplishments, he feels being kind is his most important objective.

adjectives

committed

Committed to his art, to his students, his family, his friends, *committed* feels this is the best word for him. "You can interpret 'committed' however you like," he adds with a wink.

driven

A high-achieving student, *driven* has ambitious goals, which she is driven to accomplish.

determined

Determined, an alumni director, civic leader, and mountain biker, faces all life's challenges with determined vigor. "We are constantly required to deal with changes in the world and in our lives," he relays, "many of them unfamiliar and even a little scary. Meeting those challenges head-on, making sense of them, and turning them to our advantage is the key to success and happiness."

compassionate

As a person of deep faith, *compassionate* knows that caring is at the heart of the Gospel. She consciously strives to be compassionate in all the choices she makes.

true

Lofty though this word choice may be, *true's* conviction is that being true—being loyal, and being a friend—are of ultimate importance.

musical

Musical, a music educator, sings: "Music is my spirit food. A source of joy, stress relief, and connection to my family, friends, and mostly, God, my Creator. To put it lightly, I love music!"

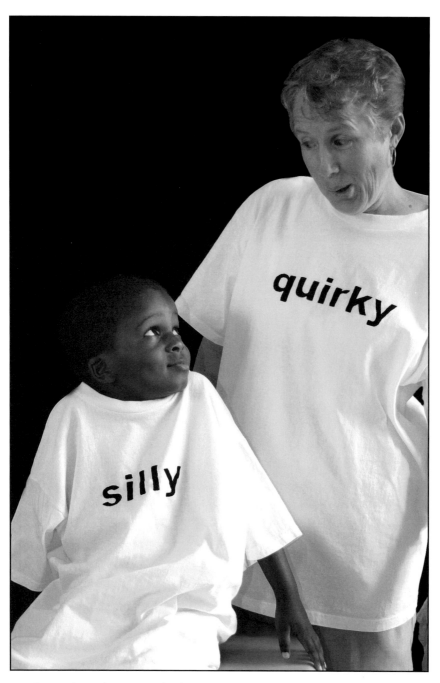

Mother and son share a quirky, but silly moment.

silly

Silly, a wise five-year-old who understands that being silly is the most serious thing a person can be, spreads joy and laughter wherever he goes. "What do you call a chorus of faucets?" he adds, then smiling, answers, "A soap opera!"

quirky

"I have always seen myself as perfectly normal," says *quirky,* "but from childhood people have told me otherwise. In youth I was odd for reading and being fascinated with ideas. This impracticality worried my father. In graduate school people marveled at what they saw as the odd conflict between my deep Roman Catholic faith and my absolute commitment to active feminism. As a professor in the Midwest my direct, unvarnished approach to telling the unpleasant historical truth was described as 'blunt and argumentative.' Amazed, I asked, 'Isn't that what the academy is all about?' And then the ultimate shock— a 42-year-old single woman adopted a newborn baby! So I choose 'quirky' to assert that other people's definitions and stereotypes about how 'certain' people 'ought' to be, don't really work in the way most people live their daily lives. Life is not coherent and we are all quirky. To be quirky is to be normal."

adverbs

extremely

Extremely, a pastor, asked a good friend to help her select her word. Her friend noted that it might sound too arrogant to pick something like "cute" or "intelligent." "But wouldn't that feel good?" she asked. "Isn't that what you want to be known as? Or better yet—how about 'extremely bright' or 'extremely beautiful' or 'extremely fun?'" They laughed over all the things they would secretly like to be called. Then in good-spirited fun, they landed at just "extremely." As a word, it makes whatever follows it become something more than it is on its own. "For me," *extremely* comments, "that is a worthy life goal: to enable those around me to be something more when we are together than any of us might be on our own."

indubitably

Indubitably says this has always been her favorite word and she was delighted to have an "indubitably" T-shirt to take home with her when she and her husband returned to India after his experience of being a visiting professor in Iowa. "Indubitably" means unquestionably, without a doubt. With all of her education, experiences, ideas, and opinions, she is undoubtedly *indubitably*.

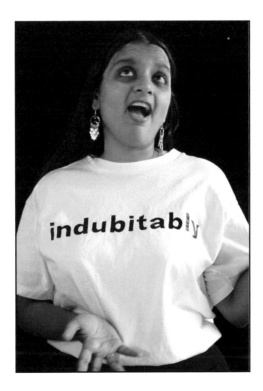

now

As a professor of dance, co-founder of a collaborative arts company, partner to one, and mother of four boys within four years, *now* survives by "being in the present!" Living the "now" of daily moments has provided her with the adrenaline and spirit necessary to embody the practice of living well with life. The flip side to this philosophy is recognizing the "now" word also functions as a command. Thus, her life is a constant balancing act of living in the now, even when her children are shouting, "NOW!"

conjunctions

but

"Generalizations polarize," explains *but,* a jazz pianist and composer. "There is always an alternative, even if we ourselves are not aware of it. 'But' gives us, at least in speech and writing, a method of expressing an alternative. This is an important option to have, especially if there is no truth whatsoever to the statement being made. I dare say "but" may be the most important conjunction out there."

or

Or is a writer, artist, and librarian who has long been troubled by choices. As a child, she made up a game called "or," which she played with her siblings. "I always seem to be caught between choices—choices of belief, choices of action, choices of being. Isn't this the human condition? It is for me. Since I can't stop playing the "or" game, I gotta believe there must be some value in the consideration of choice."

and

A photographer and pastor and writer and speaker and composer, *and* is constantly finding new things to add to his busy life and it was this very urge that sparked the initial concept for this book.

if

"If" is a powerful word indicating imagination, encouragement, hope, and infinite possibility. I am ever dreaming up a new project and bringing it to life—and it always begins with an "if."

nouns

angel

One Saturday afternoon, William and I were stranded on the side of the road with our broken-down Jeep, a 1977 CJ-7. The temperature was well over one hundred degrees and despite all the phone calls we'd made, no local mechanics would help us. We were two hours from home and needed to get back so we could preach the next day. In exasperation, we called our own mechanic. He told us to hang on, that he'd be right there.

Sure enough, two hours later, he appeared with his tool box, a trailer to tow us home if necessary, and a cooler full of cold pop to boot. "You saved the day!" I exclaimed.

"I do this all the time," he smiled. "That's why people call me the guardian angel."

color

"Color," declares *color*, "has so many connotations. It can be the color of your painting or the color of your skin. Let's use color to create, not discriminate."

bridge

Folk musician, taxi driver, and spiritual leader, *bridge* uses his energy to bridge disparate beings, histories, times, geographic locations, and ideas. "Sometimes we feel as though we are spanning a chasm," he explains of the human condition. "Other times we might be a footbridge, bringing together two different entities only an arm's length away from each other." Being a bridge can be an enormous burden, and yet he does so beautifully—dancing his worlds together and being peacemaker wherever he goes.

synergy

Born in Berlin during the bombings of WWII, *synergy* survived and migrated, through some great luck, to the U.S. "That's when I discovered the 'land of unlimited opportunity' and learned a new language," he recalls. "Over time, I also learned that the energy from two cultures can be combined into a beautifully creative force called 'synergy.' Actually, I have always enjoyed the power and pleasure of words and every day that I meet my accounting class, we choose a 'word for the day.' We always start with 'synergy.'"

nouns

fervor

Filled with enthusiasm and ready for new adventures, *fervor* now teaches English in Germany. She feels that the word "fervor" captures the energy with which she approaches her teaching as well as her life.

doer

Don't get in this journalist's way. *Doer* makes extraordinary things happen wherever she goes. "For me," she declares, "doing provides a source of satisfaction and pride as well as a knowingness that God always provides whatever is needed."

instigator

A husband, father, and Lutheran pastor, *instigator* explains, "These three vocations allow, even demand, much instigation and sometimes the instigation of mischief."

nouns

optimist

A college student from the Dominican Republic and talented pianist, *optimist* sees the bright side of every situation and approaches life with great humor.

seed

As a grower and director of a community farming cooperative, *seed* picked this word, an agricultural metaphor of her own abundant potential.

birdboy

I remember several years ago when we asked my cousin, *birdboy*, what his latest hobbies were. He was just in elementary school at the time. He listed off all the ornithological organizations of which he was a member and proceeded to show us the extensive log of birds he'd seen. Then, with a very confident look, he pronounced, "I'm the youngest birder in Iowa."

beat

"'Beat' relates to many important parts of my life," explains *beat*. "As a music enthusiast, it represents the rhythm and pulse of a song. As a reader and writer, it refers to my favorite genre of literature. Most importantly, this word defines the energy in a single heartbeat—the rhythm that keeps us alive."

bucket

This word choice started out as an inside joke between *bucket* and his college roommate, but later, as he contemplated it, he found this word actually has deeper implications. "Just as a bucket needs to be filled, I feel that as a student, I am seeking to be filled with knowledge and insights. So I guess I really am a bucket after all."

emphasis

The word "emphasis" refers to an unhalting intensity of expression that gives importance to something. As a co-founder of a farming cooperative, *emphasis* can often be found addressing organizations and individuals about the importance of community sustainable agriculture and other practices that preserve our environment.

love

Though *love* does not presume to be the embodiment of such a high ideal, her motto in life is just that: love. She believes that the absence of it causes every problem in the world. "Every life is enriched by making love speak through every action," she says, "and that's what my faith leads me to do."

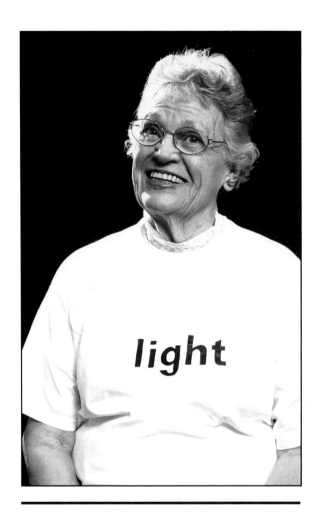

light

A delightful woman of faith, *light* proclaims, "Jesus Christ is the light of my life. I walk in that light."

passion

One professor said of *passion*, who came all the way from Zimbabwe to go to college in the Midwest, "She blossomed from being a shy and reserved young girl into a passionate advocate for woman's rights, and peace and justice issues."

believer

Believer is the former Lutheran Youth Organization president of her synod, the daughter of two Lutheran pastors, and sister of a missionary in Africa. She struggles to live out her faith in all that she does.

worship

Because faith compels him to lead a life of devotion, *worship* intends for his whole life to be an act of worship to God.

midwife

Midwife delivered more than 2,500 babies in her career as a Certified Nurse Midwife. Wherever she goes in Anchorage, Alaska, someone usually runs up to her and says, "You delivered me!" Bearing witness to the miracle of birth for so many years has given her a deep, abiding faith.

juice

A hearty distillate of life. Active, fluid, tangy, and sweet, "juice" implies impertinence, vitality, and play. She says, "Juice is perhaps what I aspire to—a life that is dynamic, vital, and richly nourishing."

bud

Experienced, self-employed mechanic and friend to all, *bud* says, "I'm just *bud*. All my life I've been a *bud*. That's why everyone out here in the country calls me *bud*."

me

Me used to be a community newspaper editor, but nowadays she spends most of her time communing with and writing about cows. "As far as 'me' goes," she says, "I think it sums me up quite nicely. It rolls all the other living words which apply to me into two little letters: M-E. That, and I think you need to be at least 30 in most cases before you know who 'me' is for you."

yin & yang

Yin and *yang* are three-year-old twin brothers whose behaviors remind their parents of the Chinese philosophy of yin and yang—an ancient understanding of the duality of life. *Yin* (the brother in the black shirt) has a more contemplative approach to life, is more passive, in touch with his emotions, is always cold, and likes to stay in bed longer, snuggling under the down comforter. Meanwhile, *yang* (in the white shirt), who has a bold, extroverted energy that unfortunately can take the form of whining and screaming, is independent, decisive, always warm, and therefore determined not to wear coats, hats, mittens, or any clothes at all—preferring to be naked whenever he can get away with it. Because these twins are such opposites, they give their mom and dad a rich, full, and sometimes exasperating parenting experience. *Yin* and *yang* are both capable, however, of flashing a smile as big as a mountain to melt any frustration away.

tranquility

Tranquility is a music professor and concert pianist from China. "Tranquility," he explains, "is an awareness of inner peace connected to the eternal, yet ever-changing world."

luther

The president of Luther College in Decorah, Iowa, chose the name of his institution to describe himself because, he explains, "for me, Luther is a 24/7/365 vocation."

listener

When asked what his living word would be, *listener* knew instantly that this was his choice because his name means "listener" in Hebrew. In his life as a pastor, professor, scholar, lecturer, and writer, he has found the most powerful ministry of all is that of listening.

helper

Helper, who has worked as a musician, teacher, massage therapist, and an activities director at a nursing care center, discovered that being a helper is the thread that ties together all her endeavors.

teacher

Teaching pervades all that *teacher* does as a professor, artist, father, and Christian. He looks to Christ as a model for teaching and recognizes that being a teacher is holy work.

father

While *father* is an innovative artist and multitalented professor, he finds his role as a father to be his most important.

troll

"Why 'troll?'" Explains theatre professor *troll* of his word choice, "Living almost forty years in Northeast Iowa, it is clear to me that trolls exist. They control the weather; they amuse themselves with bits of mischief like leaving a fence open so the cows wander into town or hiding your ice scraper in the middle of winter or inserting odd messages in your word document. They are often grumpy yet in a lovable way, creative in an offbeat manner, and zealous (especially the Swedish trolls) about playing tennis, winter or summer! So celebrating their passionate grumpiness keeps their disruption to a minimum and their frenetic energy fervently focused. Why 'troll?' I have no idea."

poetry

Poetry thinks that poems resonate deeply with our daily lives—our sorrows, joys, worries, prayers, and relationships. As a teacher, she loves guiding students to their discoveries about poems—their wit and rhetorical power, their ability to deepen our lives, to make us more human and humane. As director of Luther College's Poetry Project, she seeks to build a wider audience for poetry's power and relevance. As a poet, she works to give musical cadence to crafted lines that speak truths. And she finds poetry in both the beauty and the suffering of the world.

wonder

Wonder quotes Socrates who said, "Wisdom begins in wonder," and while she knows she has much to learn and experience before she gains the wisdom she seeks, she is reaching toward it. "In my lifetime," *wonder* says longingly, "I hope others can learn to be still and silent in wonder, gaining wisdom and peace."

remembrance

"A poem, a photo, a lasting memory. Remembrance is a key to who we are," says *remembrance,* a photographer. "My past journeys, both the good and the bad, have made my life what it is. For that I am *remembrance.*"

paperwork

As an artist whose favorite medium is handmade paper and books, *paperwork* defines her artistry and passion. Yet, as an art professor and departmental head, she also has to deal with the busy paperwork that overwhelms her and often keeps her from her artistic paperwork.

yes

A professional actor and teacher, *yes* urges her theatre students to say "yes" to new ideas and experiences. "'Yes,'" she says, "is a word that opens the door to understanding, creativity, and adventure." In her own life, she jubilantly lives out this resounding yes.

preposition

with

A PhD candidate, athlete, and avid outdoors woman, *with* finds that her connection to others is what brings the most meaning to her life. She is always doing things with friends, researching with colleagues, or adventuring in the mountains with family. During her experience as a foreign student in Germany and as a teacher for the Peace Corps in Ghana, she discovered that being with people of other cultures and backgrounds is especially enriching. "'With' is just such a great word!" she exclaims. "'With' brings the potential of two things to a higher zenith. For example, fresh raspberries are meant to go with vanilla ice cream. "

preposition

verbs

intrigue

To intrigue is to arouse the interest, desire, or curiosity of. *Intrigue* enjoys the mystery of this word and is constantly intrigued by life.

imagine

Curious and creative, *imagine* imagines a better world and is committed to being about the work of that transformation.

contemplate

Contemplate, a college registrar and associate dean, has made contemplation a way of life. He says, "I feel that we are moving too quickly nowadays, and there is a need to slow down and ponder the people we meet and events that we experience. When we move forward in time, do we know where we have been so that we understand the purpose of our next destination? And do we reflect on the gifts we have received in life and those that we shared with others? Always something to contemplate."

seeking

A photographer and recent college graduate, *seeking* has become his primary vocation—seeking religious truth, seeking understanding, and seeking a career path that's suited to his unique gifts.

becoming

Like most us of, *becoming* is still in process—recognizing that she is not yet all that she can and will be. Yet, she is actively becoming. Always finding herself in a constant state of transition, she places her current identity in her passage between childhood and adulthood, African culture and American culture, and singleness and marriage—all mirroring her life journey of becoming more like Christ.

giggle

Giggle finds joy and humor in the everyday. Once she starts to giggle, it's hard for her to stop. In fact, her unique giggle has become her trademark.

laugh

If laughter really is the best medicine, then *laugh* should be incredibly healthy. He is constantly amused and his favorite thing to do is laugh.

nurture

Nurture is a mother and active member of her church and community. Whatever is in need of nurture—be it a plant, animal, child, friend, or even a stranger—she is there to help.

hope

An English and Africana Studies professor, *hope* recognizes that hope is such a colossal concept that no one could fully embody it. Nevertheless, he exuberantly hopes and inspires others to hope for a better world for all people.

spin

College minority writer-in-residence, *spin* explains, "Sometimes words and ideas feel as though they are in some sort of a rhythmic movement like that of a dryer: something rising up, something falling, the same set of clothes in different combinations. I have always loved to dance, and spinning in its purest sense reminds me of being a child, when just spinning and then letting the world catch up with you, that blurring, that falling down on the grass, that was enough. A physical spin pushes me out of my head and into what is here now, into how we inhabit the space now. Movement into action. Motion toward rest."

moving

Moving, a dancer, a free spirit, likes the fact that this word can describe both physical movement and depth of emotion and insisted on moving as this moving portrait was taken.

shining

Nursing professor, specializing in surgical nursing and medical ethics, *shining* seeks to shine forth kindness wherever she goes. She is, indeed, a shining example of compassion.

epilogue

This project proved to be more fun than we had ever dreamed. Discussing the *Living Word* and asking people, "What one word defines you?" turned out to be a great party trick. We've found it sparks lively conversation with most everyone, especially at social gatherings. So we'd like to offer some ideas to help you ignite *Living Word* discussions of your own.

one-on-one conversations

Any conversation can move beneath the surface if you ask the other person to define him or herself in just one word. Many people are initially stumped by this question. If this is the case, ask them to begin by brainstorming possible choices. As you can see by our collection, this descriptive word can be any part of speech. Ask your friend to consider words from all these categories. Share your own word and explain why you chose it. The discussion will likely take off from there.

group conversations

Use the one-on-one guidelines to begin a *Living Word* discussion in a group setting. Ask each person to share their word or words if they are yet undecided. This can be a particularly helpful conversation in a group, for example, where people know each other but only superficially. This can open the door for more profound sharing.

party games

As we've said, you can have a lot of fun with this concept. Host your own *Living Word* party. Ask people to decide upon their word ahead of time and wear a *Living Word* T-shirt to the gathering. Custom shirts with the *Living Word* logo on the back can be ordered at www.thegentryjoint.com, or people can make their own with markers or fabric paint. Have name tags at the door so that those without T-shirts can still wear their word. Insist that no one addresses anyone else at the party by their real name—they must only use their *Living Word*. Play mixer games such as these:

- ask the group to get in a line by alphabetical order and introduce themselves to the people next to them
- have them gather in groups by parts of speech and discuss their words
- invite them to form phrases with their words
- challenge small groups to write haiku poems using their words and read them to the group
- give awards for longest word, shortest word, most creative word, etc.

Be creative and make up word games of your own. And do write and tell us about your *Living Word* festivities—better yet, send pictures. We hope these ideas will inspire fantastic parties overflowing with hilarity and meaningful dialogue.